D0549866

better **because...** of you

better
because™
of you

Ginny Hutchinson & Cathy Haffner

This is a work of nonfiction.
Some names and identifying details have been changed.

First published in 2009 by
Bending New Corners Press, LLC

With offices at:
230 – 35th Avenue East
Seattle, WA 98112
www.bendingnewcorners.com

©2009 by Virginia S. Hutchinson and Catherine Haffner

All rights reserved. No part of this publication may
be reproduced or transmitted in any form by any means,
electronic or mechanical, including photocopying,
recording, or by information storage and retrieval system,
without permission in writing from Bending New Corners
Press, LLC. Reviewers may quote brief passages.

Paperback ISBN: 978-0-9825191-0-3

Library of Congress Cataloging-in-Publication Data
#2009906789

Cover and text design by View Design Company
Edited by John Koval
Illustrations by Kath Walker
Typeset in Joanna and Officina fonts
Printed by ColorGraphics, Seattle, WA, USA, on recycled paper.

FIRST PAPERBACK EDITION

Bending New Corners
PRESS

To our families,
Bart, Blair & Lauren
Noll, Brittany, Katrina & Cassidy,
and all our many friends
who support us!

If it is
to be
it begins
with me.

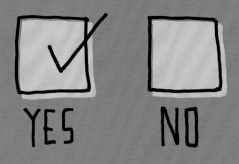

It's up to each of you to participate in life.

—HIS HOLINESS, THE 14TH DALAI LAMA,
TENZIN GYATSO, IN SEATTLE, AT SEEDS OF COMPASSION

better because... of you

WHEN WE SAW His Holiness, the Dalai Lama, he had a twinkle in his eye. He has a reputation for tickling someone who is being too serious, to get a smile or laugh. He maintains he is just an ordinary monk who is trying to make the world a little bit better.

He challenged each of us to participate in life, saying: "Every individual can make a positive difference in the world."

That changed everything for us.

We had both left our corporate jobs and were each searching for something. Then we reconnected, got together, and talked through the night. Shortly thereafter, we created Better Because, a platform for inspiring positive change through individual actions.

"If it is to be, it begins with me."

This motto works on every level. We use it to remind ourselves how we, as individuals, can make the world a little bit better.

Ginny & Cathy

cont

e n t s

3 Core Beliefs

better because...
you know

AS WE CLIMBED the corporate ladder to senior positions in Fortune 100 companies, we both went through a lot of top-rated training and executive coaching. Ginny was in marketing and Cathy was in financial services. We are fortunate that our companies invested in us, providing leadership programs that helped us achieve success in business.

After we left our jobs, we realized that these same tools worked just as well for life in general.

So we've picked the best of what we learned along the way—from executive coaches, close friends, and family—and gathered it all in this book.

3 Core Beliefs

Life Is What You Think.

Our thoughts influence our actions, which determine results.

Life Cycles.

Life is not a straight line, but a series of cycling circles.

Life's a Gem.

Life has many facets that make up the whole sparkling gem.

FIRST. Life Is What You Think.

Consider this saying from Mahatma Gandhi:

> Let your thoughts be positive
> For they will become your words.
> Let your words be positive
> For they will become your actions.
> Let your actions be positive
> For they will become your values.
> Let your values be positive
> For they will become your destiny.

Our thoughts influence our actions, which determine results. Positive thoughts lead to inspired actions, which can lead to better results.

You've probably heard this before, but it's a good reminder. If we are to make the world better, it begins with how we think.

SECOND. Life cycles.

Life doesn't follow straight lines like this:

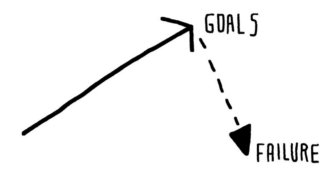

It's more like a series of circles that go around and around, up and down, like this:

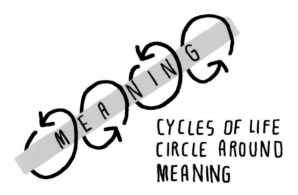

CYCLES OF LIFE
CIRCLE AROUND
MEANING

Each circle has four distinct phases:

Sometimes we may be feeling down. It's okay to start questioning what's going on in our lives. This questioning can lead to creative thinking, which leads to inspired action, and gets our life back on a positive track. If the doldrums set in again, we will languish there until we again begin questioning, which leads to creative options, which takes us once again to inspired action.

THIRD. Life's a Gem.

Most of us get caught in some sort of tunnel vision. Work, work, work. Or, everything for the kids. Or, totally sports.

But in reality life has many facets. Here are seven that seem to cover everything.

health wealth
wisdom work
others service
play

Keep all the facets in your vision all the time, and you'll see a sparkling gem that is your entire life.

These three core beliefs drive the Better Because Movement.

In order to inspire positive change through our individual actions, we try to be conscious of our thoughts, aware of life cycles, and sensitive to the phase we are in at any given time.

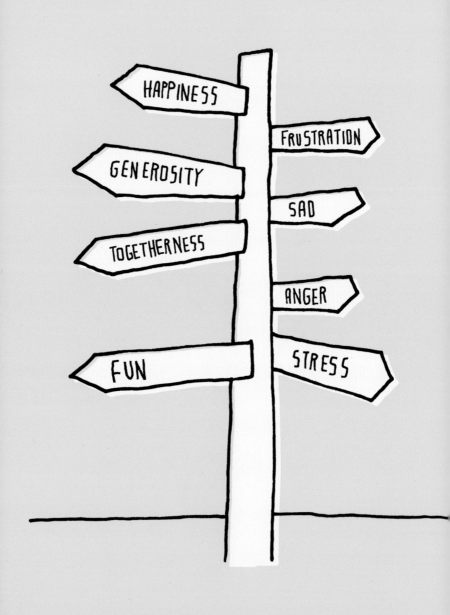

7 Facets of Life

better because...
you choose

Every day, you have a choice. Will you maintain the status quo? Or will you try to make things a little better for yourself and for others?

We've gathered a few practices for each of life's seven facets.

These exercises help us every day. They can help you bring a constant source of joy into your life. Be a happier, more inspired person, and you will make a positive difference in the world.

choose to make it better

better
because
of health

health

Moderation. Small helpings. Sample a little bit of everything.
These are the secrets of happiness and good health.

—JULIA CHILD

OUR PHYSICAL HEALTH and mental attitude are essential to everything else. Put this facet first. As the flight attendant says, "Put your oxygen mask on first before you help others."

Thrive: Don't Just Survive

If we were given a just few days to live, we would certainly use our remaining time wisely. But why wait for something like that? We can choose to start living to the fullest right now.

Marilyn: As a person who has encountered cancer twice in her life, Marilyn considers herself as a "thriver" not just a "survivor" of cancer. Rather than being a victim, she saw her experience as transformational—her cancer was an opportunity to discover the possibilities in life. Today she is a healing coach, helping people with cancer create a healing plan, and choose to take control of their lives. "Now I help others thrive, not just survive."

Start Your Day Over

If you got up on the wrong side of the bed or had an unpleasant conversation with someone, remember that you can always start your day over. Anytime you want!

Ginny: "I called in to make a dentist appointment and asked the receptionist, *How's your day going?* The receptionist said, *I'm having a really bad day.* When I suggested, *Hey, why don't you start your day over?*, the receptionist responded sarcastically: *Oh that sounds like a good idea.*

"*I'm really serious,* I insisted. *You can do it right now.*

"The receptionist paused, laughed, and her attitude changed. The rest of the conversation was lighter. She started her day all over again and thanked me."

Stand Tall

Be aware of your posture. How you sit or stand affects how you feel and those feelings are communicated to others.

Cathy: "When my posture is slumped, I feel heavy all over. The minute I hold my head high and straighten my back, my self-image and aura change. And, it makes me feel more confident. Even if you don't initially feel that way, once you project it, you become it."

Lighten Up with Laughter

Do your heart a favor and look for laughs. Share the humor with others, and hang out with friends who make you laugh (you know who they are!).

Ginny: "When I was going through the doldrums at a low point in my day, I needed an emotional lift. A good friend sent me a link to a YouTube video and by the end I was crying with hysterical laughter. This motivated me to think beyond my current situation and rejoice in simply laughing to feel better."

Rosanne & Liz: These women started a "dinner club" with other couples from their children's school. Once a month, a couple hosts the dinner and provides the main course. Everyone else brings a salad or side dish and a bottle of wine. By the end of the evening, Liz says, "there's been so much laughter; our cheeks get lots of exercise!"

Cathy: "I put together a Bunco group with other ladies in my neighborhood. We rotate houses, and everyone provides snacks, desserts, or beverages. It's a great way to get to know your friends better and have a lot of fun and laughs."

Enjoy the Silence

Make it a point to sit in silence. Center yourself. Ask about what's going on in your life. Be still and listen.

Ginny: "Nearly every day I enjoy the stillness of the morning before the buzz of the day begins. Lighting a candle. Relaxing in a quiet room. With folded hands, I spend 10 minutes meditating to start the day refreshed."

Marva: Whenever Marva needs inspiration, she takes a long walk, or finds a quiet room in her house to sit in silence. She thinks of people or things for which she is grateful, starting with "A" and going through "Z." "It's a wonderful way to step back from the rush of life and truly appreciate what blessings we have."

Look Up

Take time to be present and relish the ordinary moments of your life. Be aware of your current place, not the past or the future. This means, look up from your cell phone, laptop, or TV. See what's going on around you.

Mark: Mark is the owner of a successful film-production company. The mantra he shared with Ginny the first day he met her was, "Look up." Look up to the sky and nature, look up from texting and typing, and look up to role models. For inspiration, he looks up to the sky from his office window for quick breaks. He looks up and walks around the office, checking in with his crew. He looks up to role models in his life and others look up to him as a role model for his positive outlook on life.

Take a Hike!

Take a walk every day. Breathe in the fresh air, enjoy the scenery, and notice the wonders of nature around you.

Pam: Pam started a dog walkers group. Every morning the owners and their playful dogs walk a loop around their neighborhood and the dogs chase tennis balls in the park. Pam says, "We give the dogs exercise and love to catch up with daily news. It's a great way to be in nature, give our puppies a group outing, and visit with neighbors—all in one!"

Lauren: Lauren shared with us how she's paying attention to the changes of season more often now. From the arrival of the robins in the Spring to the changing Fall colors, she exclaims, "Nature's amazing when you take the time to notice it."

better
because
of wealth

wealth

A big part of financial freedom is having your heart and mind free from worry about the what-ifs of life.

—SUZE ORMAN

THIS LIFE FACET is the cause of anxiety for many, no matter what their financial situation. Try these suggestions to enjoy the fruits of your labor.

Spend. Save. Give.

Make sure each dollar earned is split among these three uses: spend a certain amount, save a portion, and always remember to give.

Lalie: Lalie is the creator of the Moonjar Moneybox, a teaching bank with three compartments for saving, spending, and sharing. The Moonjar encourages children and families to set goals, spend wisely, and impact their community in lasting ways. It's a great learning tool that applies at every age. If you spend 80%, sock away 15% and give 5%, no matter what your income level, you'll be using a disciplined approach to managing what you earn.

Live Within Your Means

Achieve independence by limiting your consumption, especially when buying on credit. Ask yourself: *Can we pay cash or use a debit card instead?*

Tom: When Cathy worked in a bank branch, Tom applied for a debt consolidation loan. Tom's family had racked up a large sum in debt from various credit cards. The bank approved them for a home equity loan with a lower interest rate and even lower monthly payments. With the money they saved, Tom was able to begin saving for his children's college fund. "It's a big sense of relief to be on a better path, managing my credit and now saving for the future."

Earn More from Your Work

If you or your partner work for a U.S. company with a 401k Plan, consider signing up as soon as you're eligible. It's a popular retirement plan with free money from your employer, and may lower your taxable income.

Cathy: "From my experience working for different U.S. financial companies, I was surprised to see how many employees could participate, yet didn't. In some companies, for every dollar you contribute from your salary, your employer matches another dollar in the fund up to a certain percent. It's a great way to double your savings for retirement, earn more from your company, and automatically save every month without any effort."

Decide What's Enough

Take the time to figure out what's sufficient for you to live a fulfilling life. Ask yourself: *How much do we really need?*

Cathy & Ginny: "When we worked in banking, we met many

7 Facets of Life

people extending themselves on credit, while they had very little savings. We learned early on to ask, *Do I really need this?* before making big purchases. We took active management of our finances each month to ensure we were on-track with our saving and spending goals.

"For us, managing finances is a constant activity that's never done. Whether it's saving for your nest egg or helping your children understand trade-offs, it's a series of ongoing decisions."

better
because
of wisdom

wisdom

People are like stained-glass windows. They sparkle and shine when the sun is out, but when the darkness sets in, their true beauty is revealed only if there is a light from within.

—ELISABETH KÜBLER-ROSS

THIS ASPECT OF LIFE completes the old saying, "Healthy, wealthy, and wise." But wisdom is more than aging, and more than knowledge. It encompasses mental, spiritual, and emotional awareness.

Find a Gratitude Object

Find a stone or special object that you can keep with you during the day. Each time you hold it, think of something you appreciate—whether it's someone in your life or something good that happened.

Cassidy: Cassidy took a jewelry-making class at a local school. She made herself a bracelet with three beads. She wears the bracelet to remind herself there are at least three people or things in her life that make her happy every day.

"There are times when the day is challenging," says Cassidy. "So I reach over to the bracelet, touch a bead, and feel gratitude. Sometimes I think of someone who did something nice that day. At the very least, I can be thankful for being alive and breathing!"

Mik: Mik recently got engaged. His bride-to-be gave him a red, heart-shaped stone that he keeps in his pocket every day. It's a constant reminder of their love and commitment to one another.

Just Name It

Recognize what's happening with yourself during the day. What emotions are you feeling? If you're sad or upset, it's okay. What's important is that you recognize where you are, which will help uncover your true state of being.

John: This life coach calls it, "Just Name It, Dude." John encourages people to check in daily with their feelings or issues by sharing them with another person. It's a great way to be more self-aware, connected with others, and to have fun in the process.

Make Time to Meditate

You don't need to take a course, although it helps. Just make some time every day—even five minutes—to unplug and

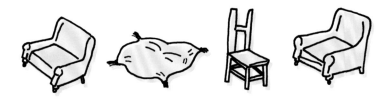

recharge. Simply be alone, sit still, and quiet your thoughts. You'll be surprised at how that changes you.

Katie: Katie often starts her day with a few minutes of meditation. She sits quietly, when everyone else is asleep, closes her eyes, and thinks of a single word like "love" to find inner peace before her day begins. Sometimes she takes an early morning walk, with the same restorative effect.

Robert: When Robert needs to refocus, he finds a quiet spot and thinks about his favorite vacation place. It's usually the beach, with the sound of the ocean providing a soothing environment. "It's amazing how this 'mental vacation' helps relax me, to get through a tough day."

Read Words from the Wise

You can always get a lift by reading or sharing famous quotes, moving poems, or inspiring parables. We assembled a collection for your daily reference in the back of this book.

Joe: Joe and his team attended a leadership program that was spread out over the course of a year. The participants were asked to choose a poem or quote that best described them. He chose this passage by George Bernard Shaw and he rereads it whenever he needs a source of inspiration:

This is the true joy in life, the being used for a purpose recognized by yourself as a mighty one; the being thoroughly worn out before you are thrown on the scrap heap; the being a force of Nature instead of a feverish, selfish little clod of ailments and grievances complaining that the world will not devote itself to making you happy.

I am of the opinion that my life belongs to the whole community, and as long as I live it is my privilege to do for it whatever I can.

I want to be thoroughly used up when I die, for the harder I work, the more I live. I rejoice in life for its own sake. Life is no brief candle to me; it is a sort of splendid torch which I have got a hold of for the moment, and I want to make it burn as brightly as possible before handing it on to future generations.

—GEORGE BERNARD SHAW

Pretend You're 90

Look back on your life as if you're 90 years old. What made you proud? What did you do with the years of your life? Imagining you're 90, list all the things you're most happy about and grateful for. How does this new view change your decisions today?

Ginny: "Growing up in a military family, I knew I wanted to enjoy a stint abroad with my own family. It was hard deciding the timing, how it would work, and what country to live in. Then, I just decided one day to start taking action. I discussed my dream more openly, which eventually led to hearing about a position in London and one in São Paulo and getting offered both. We chose London and our family enjoyed five years of living and travel abroad and never looked back."

better
because
of work

work

To love what you do and feel that it matters—
how could anything be more fun?

—KATHARINE GRAHAM

THE IMPORTANT THING to remember with this facet is that it is only ONE of SEVEN facets that make up our life.

Write a "Better" Letter

Date a letter one year from today and write in detail about all the accomplishments you hope to achieve. Write as if they all have happened, and congratulate yourself for your success. Always include a personal goal, outside of work. Don't hold back—shoot for the moon.

Rina: As part of Cathy's annual goal-setting, she asked her team to create a letter that defined business and personal goals. Rina's goals included her marketing and business plans, and having her paintings displayed in a New York City gallery. "When I set these goals, I had no idea how or when they would happen," Rina recalls. "Within a few months, I achieved both. I was skeptical at first of the exercise, but am now a strong believer and use it with my own team."

State Your Intentions

When starting a new project, write down details of what you want to accomplish. Consider all the possible ways to reach the goal. Include key stakeholders who can help you get there.

Bruce: Bruce applies this concept to many areas in his life, from fitness to business goals. As the CEO, he set a stretch goal to achieve $66 million in revenue by the end of the year. So he asked Ginny to create a Route 66 theme with posters, progress reports "along the highway," and T-shirts. Employees wore them every Friday until they surpassed the goal. Not only was it a visible sign of teamwork and goal setting, everyone had a lot of fun and laughs along the way.

Create a Visualization Board

Buy a blank poster board. Think about your life one to two years from now. Cut out and paste up pictures from magazines or download images from the Internet that represent your dreams: key relationships, a dream home, education, charities to support, vacation destinations, or hobbies that interest you.

Raj: Raj attended a leadership program where he created a visualization board. He was unsatisfied with his job and wanted to make better use of his time and talents. "I found a picture of a leading technology company with energetic people. Within a year, I had my dream job. It was absolutely unreal."

Make Social Connections

Research demonstrates that the most satisfied people at work are those who have a best friend there. If you don't have one, look around. It's the place where you spend much of your time. It's helps to have someone close you can confide in or let off some steam with when needed.

Ginny & Cathy: "Early on in our careers, we joined our work friends for regular social hours, potlucks, and group lunches. Even though the work was demanding, our fondest memories were the fun times we shared. This is where our friendship began. Though we went down separate paths for awhile, today, 20 years later, we've been able to reconnect and are now building Better Because together."

better
because
· · · · · · · · · · · · · ·
of play

play

*Every day brings a chance for you to draw in a breath,
kick off your shoes, and dance.*

—OPRAH WINFREY

PLAY IS OFTEN MISTAKEN for goofing off. However, taking time to relax and enjoy various hobbies and interests is an excellent change of pace and provides nourishment to the soul.

Listen to Uplifting Music

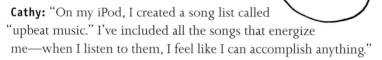

Look through your music library. Put together a playlist with music to lighten your mood, relax, or give you energy. Find "your song"—one that is a reflection of you.

Cathy: "On my iPod, I created a song list called "upbeat music." I've included all the songs that energize me—when I listen to them, I feel like I can accomplish anything."

Explore

In a survey of people toward the end of their lives, they were asked what they would have done differently. No one mentioned working harder. Instead the common themes were spending more time with loved ones, traveling, or taking more risks.

Ginny: "I'm the person who has my bags packed, ready to go. My travels have included backpacking through Europe, exploring the Pyramids with Bart when Blair and Lauren were toddlers, and a photo-safari in the Serengeti Plains when the kids were middle schoolers. We as a family like to explore the mountains and islands close to our Seattle home. Day trips like this build togetherness, are easy, and barely cost anything."

Write It Down

Find a place to write down your thoughts. List what you are grateful for. Write about what's right and not right in your life today. Ask yourself, *What would make me five percent happier?* Write down the answers.

Niki: Journaling can be done in many forms. But the one Niki likes most is called "flow writing." The purpose is to get thoughts on paper each day. She writes three full pages and never picks the pen up from the paper. Inevitably, the thoughts she started with are different from the ones at the end. After writing, she doesn't review her thoughts, but lets them be "as they are." The flow writing helps her uncover what might be on her mind at a subconscious level and bring it out. She says, "Just letting my thoughts pour out helps me be more balanced and centered for the day."

Exercise Your Creativity

Everyone can benefit from a creative outlet. Enjoy the feeling of accomplishment when you use your hands to build something lasting, tackle a crossword puzzle, play an instrument, or simply create a special meal.

Annie: Annie enjoys the art of jewelry design. From finding special stones and one-of-a-kind charms, to bending wire, then selling her jewelry to enthusiastic buyers, she enjoys the whole process. "My work is such a personal and often joyful process, it's a real labor of love. The icing on the cake is seeing people connect with it and be so happy when they're wearing it."

Luis: Landscaping is both a creative hobby and mental escape for Luis. Digging the dirt, pruning back trees, and watching the garden constantly change give him great pleasure. He exclaims, "My garden is both a thing of beauty and source of happiness for me."

Steve: Early in life, Steve played in a touring rock band and later became a corporate attorney. "I'm a rock star who became an attorney, not an attorney who plays in a band." While he's always pressed for time, he creates space for his musical passion. Steve brings a wonderful sense of humor and creativity to whatever stage he's on.

better
because
of others

others

*After God created the world, he made man and woman. Then,
to keep the whole thing from collapsing, he invented humor.*

—GUILLERMO MORDILLO

WE SOMETIMES take others in our life for granted. Pay attention and be present to those closest to you, for they can often be the source of your greatest joy and happiness.

Smile, It's Contagious

Have you ever walked down the street or ridden an elevator, and noticed how many people are looking down or have a distant look? Try this fun game to pass on a smile.

John: On their way to an event, John challenged Ginny to see how many smiles they could coax out of people along the way. He called this game, "target practice." Target someone, share a smile. "It was surprising how hard it was to get someone's attention, yet immensely rewarding getting a smile in return."

Being There

There are times when a family member or friend needs your undivided attention. All they need is for you to be there and allow them to share whatever is on their mind. Being a good listener is essential to being a better companion.

Brittany: "Every once in a while I come home from school, and it's cool that my Mom stops what she's doing and sits down with me for a snack. It lets me unwind and share the challenges or excitement from my day. I like it best when she just listens and doesn't give me advice."

Ginny: "A lingering death is never easy to face. My parents were both facing a serious illness and the last breaths of their life, so I decided to be there. Whether I was stroking my Mom's hair, silently holding my Dad's hand, or singing or reading aloud, it was about just being there. It's appreciating precious human life that's fleeting and accepting that death, too, is a part of life."

Better Family Time

Designate a time for regular family activities or a "date night" with your spouse or significant other.

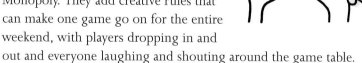

David & Cindy: David travels for his job, often for several days at a time. When he's home, one of the family's favorite activities is to play board games, like Monopoly. They add creative rules that can make one game go on for the entire weekend, with players dropping in and out and everyone laughing and shouting around the game table.

Cathy: Every week Cathy and Noll have a date night and go to their favorite restaurant. They make a conscious decision to not discuss the kids or the "to do" list, so they have time to be a couple.

Make "Popcorn"

Share each other's "special gifts" just like making popcorn—"pop" out the qualities you appreciate about that person. Use words such as: loyal friend, dedicated parent, patient teacher, or fun-loving adventurer.

Aaron: "I've used this technique with some of my best friends. The important thing is: If you're the receiver of compliments, let it soak in. I really appreciated how others perceive me. I heard things I didn't realize and I loved paying compliments in return."

Console Survivors

One of the most important times to be supportive is when a friend or family member experiences the passing of someone dear. Rather than ask, *What can I do?* say, *Here's what I will do for you.*

Pete: Pete's wife, Marianne, died suddenly, without warning. She was only 39 and they had a toddler. The neighborhood worked together to bring meals to Pete for several weeks. While Pete was planning the funeral, Marianne's "Mommy & Me" group took turns babysitting, so he had time to deal with the arrangements and spend time with relatives who were arriving.

"I was in a state of shock and denial for several days, even months, after my wife's passing," Pete recalls. "It was a relief to have such great support from friends without asking. I am eternally grateful for all their help."

Take a Stand & Set Boundaries

In relationships, the giving and taking can sometimes be out of balance. Be aware of your role in relationships—and your impact on others. First, identify where you stand for yourself. Then articulate your stand with others and set clear boundaries.

Ginny: Little did we know that the kids and I were taking advantage of Bart. When any emergency arose, like forgetting homework or dry cleaning, we relied on him to do our dirty work. Bart took a stand and, thanks to him, we've set boundaries within our family. He explained to us that he had to drop everything on his list to rush to our needs. By bringing this to our attention, we worked together to be more thoughtful and self-sufficient.

Forgive Yourself & Others

This may be challenging for anyone, though it's probably one of the most important areas for letting go of your past.

Barbara: "This story begins with you. The way you talk to yourself is probably harsher than anyone else would be. Your internal dialogue can run the gamut—commenting on your weight, looks, intellect, lack of discipline, lack of resources— you name it. This negative talk is destructive. Instead, be gentle to yourself. Be kind, patient and understanding to yourself as you are to a child or friend. Say to yourself, ... *I am enough... I have enough... I love myself... I love my life.* It's a struggle to keep this clear every day, but a helpful reminder for me."

better
because
of service

service

If you can't do great things, do small things in a great way.
Don't wait for great opportunities. Seize the common,
everyday ones, and make them great.

—NAPOLEON HILL

ONE OF THE GREATEST sources of satisfaction in life is serving
others. It's rewarding to be connected to something bigger
than yourself. They say no one has become poor by giving. And
remember, service isn't separate from the rest of your life—
rather, it is how you lead your life.

Better Community

There are many ways to serve your community, through
offering time, money, or donated goods. Choose a charity you
like or find a place that needs your talents.

Audrey: Audrey volunteered at a free summer-school
program. "I found the most rewarding part was
watching the kids' grades improve over
the summer, instead of forgetting what
they learned during the school year."

Taylor: This seven year old decided to
collect and sell used books and donate all the
money to a local food bank. After four years, he donated thou-
sands of dollars to help feed needy people in his community.

Ruanda: Ruanda struggled to rebuild her life after suffering several bouts of homelessness until she discovered the Path with Art program. There she took a free poetry class, and rediscovered her gift as a writer. "Poetry literally saved my life," she says. She is now attending community college, and plans to earn her master's degree and become a librarian.

Deborah: Using her own passion for art, Deborah filled a need in the lives of previously homeless adults. She founded Path with Art, a nonprofit organization that uses the creative process as a tool to heal others in times of crisis. Her great act of service helped Ruanda, and many like her, reconnect with the dreams they had lost *Poetry* and find their voices along the way.

Leave It Better Than You Found It

Be kind to our planet. Make your impact a positive one. Make sure you're giving more than you're taking.

Katrina: Katrina is part of Junior ROTC at her high school. Once a week, the students volunteer to collect recyclable paper from around the school. They are committed to helping the community be more eco-friendly.

Dirk: A river-rafting guide and owner, Dirk ensures that he and his guests enjoy and respect the wilderness. Every day and night guests pick up all "micro-trash," even if it was left by other people. This helps the wilderness look as unspoiled as if no human had ever been there.

Tom: Tom's work team decided to help an inner-city first-grade class with a fun group activity. Partnering with a local bookstore, they donated enough money to provide each student with three books. "Between reading the students a story and seeing the twinkle in their eyes when choosing their favorite books, this was the best team experience we've ever had."

A Better World

It's up to each of us—as individuals—to make the world a better place. You don't have to be a superhero. You can make a difference if you make better choices.

Alice: One day an older woman came into Alice's knitting shop and was surprisingly rude and ornery. The store policy is to handle these situations with kindness, which usually works, but not this time. The woman even started personally insulting the staff, yet they persisted with kindness. Two days later, the customer came back with flowers, an apology, and hugs all around. Turns out her terminal cancer medication had mental side effects. She shook her head saying, "I'm so terribly sorry how oddly I was behaving. I just felt out of sorts and I appreciate how nice you were in spite of my own frustrations."

Ginny & Cathy: "In addition to building this positive movement, our ultimate dream is to start the Better Because Foundation. We'd like to better lives around the world through education. You are already a part of this effort simply by supporting us and investing in your continuous growth. We are deeply grateful for your support and thank you for taking inspired action in your life."

Everyone: Share your "Life is Better Because…" story with others at www.BetterBecause.com.

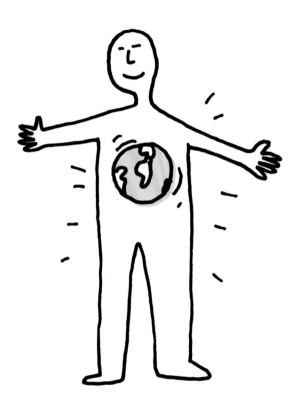

THE WORLD IS IN YOU

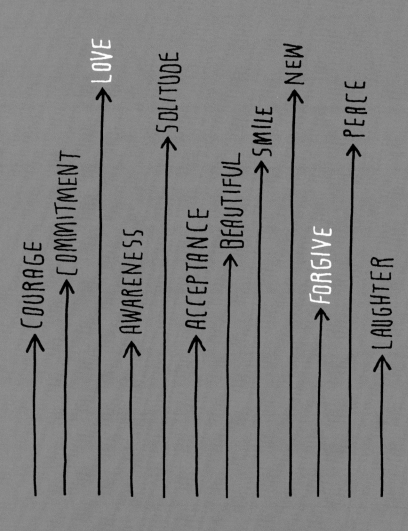

words to live by

better because...
you're inspired

When we find ourselves needing a lift, or seeking helpful words for a friend, we look through famous sayings and meaningful quotes. Brilliant people have tackled the same situations before us and come up with thoughts that inspire us all.

We're pleased to share this collection of our all-time favorites, and hope you'll find it useful in all facets of your life.

Quotes Poems
NOBODY SAID IT BETTER
Messaging
A to Z

Abundance

One cannot collect all the beautiful shells on the beach.

> —*Anne Morrow Lindbergh*

Acceptance

It takes courage to grow up and turn out to be who you really are.

> —*e.e. cummings*

The world is not out there—the world is in you.

> —*Sarah Susanka*

Achievement

The greater danger for most of us is not that our aim is too high and we miss it, but that it is too low and we reach it.

> —*Michelangelo*

Action

Yesterday is ashes; tomorrow wood. Only today does the fire burn brightly.

> —*Eskimo Proverb*

We are what we repeatedly do.

> —*Aristotle*

Do more than belong: participate.
Do more than care: help.
Do more than believe: practice.
Do more then be fair: be kind.
Do more than forgive: forget.
Do more than dream: work.

> —*William Arthur Ward*

Adventure

Because of our routines, we forget that life is an ongoing adventure.

> —*Maya Angelou*

Adversity

A successful man is one who can lay a firm foundation with bricks that others throw at him.

> —*David Brinkley*

Age

Old indeed! There's many a good tune played on an old fiddle.

> —*Samuel Butler*

Ambition

Many of life's failures occur when people give up without realizing how close they are to success.

>   —Unknown

Anger

Keep your mouth shut when you are swimming and when you are angry.

>   —Unknown

Anticipation

It is no use to wait for your ship to come in, unless you have sent one out.

>   —Belgian Proverb

Arguments

I don't have to attend every argument I'm invited to.

>   —W. C. Fields

Aspiration

A man's reach should exceed his grasp, or what's a heaven for?

>   —Robert Browning

Attitude

Your living is determined not so much by what life brings to you... as by the attitude you bring to life.

>   —John Homer Mills

Awakening

There is only one time when it is essential to awaken. That time is now.

—*Buddha*

Awareness

To become different from what we are, we must have some awareness of what we are.

—*Eric Hoffer*

Balance

I always try to balance the light with the heavy—a few tears of human spirit in with the sequins and the fringes.

—*Bette Midler*

Beginnings

The journey of a thousand miles begins with one step.

—*Lao Tzu*

Today is a new day. You will get out of it just what you put into it.

—*Mary Pickford*

Believe

It's not what you are that holds you back, it's what you think you are not.

—*Denis Waitley*

If you believe in your heart that you are right, you must fight with all your might to do it your way. Only dead fish swim with the stream all the time.

—Linda Ellerbee

Birthdays

Birthdays are to cherish and celebrate that your life makes a difference.

—Ginny Hutchinson

Boldness

Be bold. If you're going to make an error, make it a doozy, and don't be afraid to hit the ball.

—Billie Jean King

Breakthrough

I always wondered why somebody doesn't do something about that. Then I realized I was somebody.

—Lily Tomlin

Broken Heart

The soul would have no rainbow if the eyes had no tears.

—Native American saying

Business

It is amazing what you can accomplish if you do not care who gets the credit.

—Harry S. Truman

A leader's role is to raise people's aspirations for what they can become, and to release their energies so they will try to get there.

—David Gergen

Celebration

I celebrate myself, and sing myself.

—Walt Whitman

Challenges

Opportunities to find deeper powers within ourselves come when life seems most challenging.

—Joseph Campbell

A bend in the road is not the end of the road, as long as you make the turn.

—Unknown

Change

Blessed are the flexible, for they shall not be bent out of shape.

—Unknown

They say that time changes things, but you actually have to change them yourself.

—Andy Warhol

It is not the strongest of the species that survive, nor the most intelligent, but the ones most responsive to change.

      —*Charles Darwin*

Character

Faced with crisis, the man of character falls back on himself. He imposes his own stamp of action, takes responsibility for it, makes it his own.

      —*Charles de Gaulle*

Charity

If you can't do great things, do small things in a great way. Don't wait for great opportunities. Seize common, everyday ones, and make them great.

      —*Napoleon Hill*

Cheer

The best way to cheer yourself up is to try to cheer somebody else up.

      —*Mark Twain*

Children

Your children need your presence more than your presents.

      —*Jesse Jackson*

Choices

Challenge can be stepping stones or stumbling blocks—it's just a matter of how you view them.

      —*Unknown*

words to live by

It is not our abilities that determine who we are, it's our choices.

> —Dumbledore, from Harry Potter and the Chamber of Secrets
> by J. K. Rowling

Commitment

Success seems to be largely a matter of hanging on after others have let go.

> —William Feather

Find something that you're really interested in doing in your life. Pursue it, set goals, and commit yourself to excellence. Do the best you can.

> —Chris Evert

Communication

Tact is the knack of making a point without making an enemy.

> —Sir Isaac Newton

Community

Never doubt that a small group of thoughtful, committed citizens can change the world. Indeed, it is the only thing that ever has.

> —Margaret Mead

Compromise

Compromise: An amiable arrangement between husband and wife whereby they agree to let her have her own way.

> —Unknown

Making an issue of little things is one of the surest ways to spoil happiness. One's personal pride is felt to be vitally injured by surrender, but there is no quality of human nature so nearly royal as the ability to yield gracefully. It shows small confidence in one's own nature to fear that compromise lessens self-control. To consider constantly the comfort and happiness of another is not a sign of weakness but of strength.

—*Charles Conrad*

Compassion

If you want others to be happy, practice compassion. If you want to be happy, practice compassion.

—*His Holiness, the 14th Dalai Lama, Tenzin Gyatso*

Competition

Don't bother just to be better than your contemporaries or predecessors. Try to be better than yourself.

—*William Faulkner*

Compliment

I can live for two months on a good compliment.

—*Mark Twain*

Contact

People, more than things, have to be restored, renewed, revived, reclaimed, and redeemed; never throw out anyone.

—*Audrey Hepburn*

words to live by

Confidence

Somehow I can't believe that there are any heights that can't
be scaled by a man who knows the secret of making his dreams
come true. This special secret, it seems to me, can be summa-
rized in four C's. They are curiosity, confidence, courage, and
constancy, and the greatest of these is confidence. When you
believe in a thing, believe in it all the way.

—*Walt Disney*

Conflict

Conflict cannot survive without your participation.

—*Wayne Dryer*

Courage

Courage is the art of being the only one who knows you're
scared to death.

—*Earl Wilson*

Creativity

Imagination is the beginning of creation. You imagine what you
desire, you will what you imagine and at last you create what
you will.

—*George Bernard Shaw*

One ought, every day at least, to hear a little song, read a good
poem, see a fine picture and, if possible, speak a few reasonable
words.

—*Johann Wolfgang von Goethe*

Every child is an artist. The problem is how to remain an artist once he grows up.

—*Pablo Picasso*

Cry

A good cry lightens the heart.

—*Yiddish Proverb*

Dance

Every day brings a chance for you to draw in a breath, kick off your shoes, and dance.

—*Oprah Winfrey*

Dare

In this world there is always danger for those who are afraid of it.

—*George Bernard Shaw*

Decisions

Never cut a tree down in the wintertime. Never make a negative decision in the low time. Never make your most important decisions when you are in your worst moods. Wait. Be patient. The storm will pass. The spring will come.

—*Robert H. Schuller*

Death

Rather than mourn the absence of the flame, let us celebrate how brightly it burned.

—*Unknown*

So long as the memory of certain beloved friends lives in my heart, I shall say that life is good.

—*Helen Keller*

What the heart once owned and had it shall never lose.

—*Henry Ward Beecher*

Death is extraordinarily like life when we know how to live. You cannot live without dying. You cannot live if you do not die psychologically every minute.

—*Krishnamurti*

Seeing death as the end of life is like seeing the horizon as the end of the ocean.

—*David Searls*

You can shed tears that she is gone,
or you can smile because she lived.
You can close your eyes and pray that she'll come back,
or you can open your eyes and see all she's left.
Your heart can be empty because you can't see her,
or you can be full of the love you shared.
You can turn your back on tomorrow, and live yesterday,
or you can be happy for tomorrow because of yesterday.
You can remember her only that she is gone,
or you can cherish her memory and let it live on.

You can cry and close your mind,
be empty and turn your back.
Or you can do what she'd want:
smile, open your eyes, love and go on.

—David Harkins

Defeat

Never confuse a single defeat with a final defeat.

—F. Scott Fitzgerald

Despair

When you get to the end of your rope, tie a knot
and hang on!

—Franklin D. Roosevelt

Destiny

Destiny is not a matter of chance, it is a matter of choice.

—W. J. Bryan

Determination

You've got to get up every morning with determination if you're
going to go to bed with satisfaction.

—George Horace Lorimer

The difference between the impossible and the possible lies in a
person's determination.

—Tommy Lasorda

Difficulties

Out of difficulties grow miracles.

> —*La Bruyere*

Disappointment

Life can only disappoint you if you let it.

> —*Mark Hopkins*

Diversity

Diversity is the one true thing we all have in common. Celebrate it everyday.

> —*Unknown*

It takes all kinds.

> —*Unknown*

Dream

Let go of the past and go for the future… Live the life you imagined.

> —*Henry David Thoreau*

The minute you settle for less than you deserve, you get even less than you settled for.

> —*Maureen Dowd*

Duty

Keep doing good deeds long enough and you'll probably turn out a good man in spite of yourself.

> —*Louis Auchincloss*

Ego

Avoid having your ego so close to your position that when your position falls, your ego goes with it.

—Colin Powell

Energy

I ask not for a lighter burden but for broader shoulders.

—Jewish Proverb

Enthusiasm

If you aren't fired with enthusiasm, you will be fired with enthusiasm.

—Vince Lombardi

Exercise

Chop your own wood and it will warm you twice.

—Henry Ford

The sovereign invigorator of the body is exercise.

—Thomas Jefferson

Expectations

Treat a man as he is, he will remain so. Treat a man the way he can be and ought to be, and he will become as he can be and should be.

—Johann Wolfgang Goethe

Experience

Experience is not what happens to you; it what you do with
what happens to you.

>   — *Aldous Huxley*

Explore

Explore your mind, discover yourself,
then give the best that is in you... There
are heroic possibilities waiting to be
discovered in every person.

>   — *Wilfred Peterson*

Failure

I honestly think it is better to be a failure at something you love
than to be a success at something you hate.

>   — *George Burns*

I have not failed. I've just found 10,000 ways that won't work.

>   — *Thomas Edison*

You always pass failure on the way to success.

>   — *Mickey Rooney*

Faith

Not truth, but faith it is that keeps the world alive.

>   — *Edna St. Vincent Millay*

Believe in something larger than yourself.

> —*Barbara Bush*

Family

Treat your family like friends and your friends like family.

> —*Proverb*

You don't choose your family. They are God's gift to you, as you are to them.

> —*Archbishop Desmond Tutu*

Happiness is having a large, loving, caring, close-knit family in another city.

> —*George Burns*

To us, family means putting your arms around each other and being there.

> —*Barbara Bush*

Fate

Sometimes our fate resembles a fruit tree in winter. Who would think that those branches would turn green again and blossom, but we hope it, we know it.

> —*Johann Wolfgang von Goethe*

Fault

Don't find fault, find a remedy.

> —*Henry Ford*

words to live by

Fear

Decide that you want it more than you are afraid of it.

> —*Bill Cosby*

Feedback

Criticism, like rain, should be gentle enough to nourish a man's growth without destroying his roots.

> —*Frank A. Clark*

Focus

The world makes way for the man who knows where he is going.

> —*Ralph Waldo Emerson*

Forgiveness

To forgive but not forget is like burying the hatchet with the handle sticking out.

> —*Unknown*

Forgiveness means letting go of the past.

> —*Gerald Jamposky*

Always forgive your enemies—nothing annoys them so much.

> —*Oscar Wilde*

Fortune

In misfortune, lies good fortune.

> —*Unknown*

Friendship

A true friend is someone who thinks that you are a good egg even though he knows that you are slightly cracked.

—*Bernard Meltzer*

A real friend is one who walks in when the rest of the world walks out.

—*Walter Winchell*

A friend knows the song in my heart and sings it to me when my memory fails.

—*Donna Roberts*

Each friend represents a world in us, a world possibly not born until they arrive.

—*Anais Nin*

Fun

The most wasted of all days is one without laughter.

—*e.e. cummings*

If you never did, you should. These things are fun and fun is good.

—*Dr. Seuss*

Future

The best thing about the future is that it comes only one day at a time.

—*Abraham Lincoln*

Generosity

There's no traffic on the extra mile.

—*Rickey Minor*

Gifts

What you are is God's gift to you, and what you do with what you are is your gift to God.

—*George Foster*

I've learned that people will forget what you said, people will forget what you did, but people will never forget how you made them feel.

—*Maya Angelou*

Giving

It is one thing to be gifted and quite another thing to be worthy of one's own gift.

—*Nadia Boulanger*

God gives the nuts, but He does not crack them.

—*German Proverb*

Goal

I always wanted to be somebody, but I should have been more specific.

—*Lily Tomlin*

You will never reach great heights with your hands in your pockets.

> — Roger Crawford

Everything starts with yourself—with you making up your mind about what you're going to do with your life.

> — Tony Dorsett

Goodness

A good head and a good heart are always a formidable combination.

> — Nelson Mandela

Goodness is easier to recognize than to define.

> — W. H. Auden

Gratitude

Life is ten percent what you make it, and ninety percent how you take it.

> — Irving Berlin

If you have something to say to a loved one, don't wait until tomorrow. Too late comes sooner than later.

> — Nick Welton

Live every day with an attitude of gratitude.

> — Tony Robbins

Growth

There is nothing like returning to a place that remains
unchanged to find the ways in which you yourself have altered.

—*Nelson Mandela*

Happiness

Happiness and love are just a choice away.

—*Leo Buscaglia*

The road to happiness is always under construction.

—*Unknown*

Happiness is a perfume you cannot pour on others without
getting a few drops on yourself.

—*Ralph Waldo Emerson*

Now and then it's good to pause in our pursuit of happiness and
just be happy.

—*Guillaume Apollinaire*

Harmony

He who lives in harmony with himself lives in harmony with
the universe.

—*Marcus Aurelius*

Healing

Though no one can go back and make a brand new start, anyone can start from now and make a brand new ending.

—*Carl Bard*

Health

Health is not just the absence of a disease. It's an inner joyfulness that should be ours all the time, a state of positive well-being.

—*Deepak Chopra*

Moderation. Small helpings. Sample a little bit of everything. These are the secrets of happiness and good health.

—*Julia Child*

Heart

Write it in your heart that every day is the best day of the year.

—*Ralph Waldo Emerson*

Help

When a friend is in trouble, don't annoy him by asking if there is anything you can do. Think up something appropriate and do it.

—*E. W. Howe*

Home

Do not keep anything in your home that you do not know to be useful, or believe to be beautiful.

—*William Morris*

Hope

A single sunbeam is enough to drive away any shadows.

> —*Saint Francis of Assisi*

Hope costs nothing.

> —*Colette*

Humility

Humility is the only true wisdom by which we prepare our minds for all the possible changes of life.

> —*George Arliss*

Humor

A person without humor is like a car without shock absorbers.

> —*Unknown*

A sense of humor is part of the art of leadership, of getting along with people, of getting things done.

> —*Dwight D. Eisenhower*

Common sense and a sense of humor are the same thing, moving at different speeds. A sense of humor is just common sense, dancing.

> —*William James*

Honesty

Honesty is the first chapter in the book of wisdom.

> —*Thomas Jefferson*

Ideals

Ideals are like the stars; we never reach them, but like the mariners of the sea, we chart our course by them.

—*Carl Schurz*

Ideas

The best way to predict the future is to create it.

—*Peter F. Drucker*

The distance between you and dreams is often the length of a single idea.

—*Vic Conant*

Imagination

Imagination is the highest kite that one can fly.

—*Lauren Bacall*

Imagination is more important than knowledge.

—*Albert Einstein*

Individuality

Don't be afraid to be different.

—*Unknown*

You have two choices in life: You can dissolve into the mainstream or you can be distinct… To be distinct, you must be different, you must strive to be what no one else but you can be.

    — Alan Ashley-Pitt

Inferiority

No one can make you feel inferior without your consent.

    — Eleanor Roosevelt

Inspiration

Enthusiasm is the inspiration of everything great.

    — Christian Nestell Bovee

Intuition

You have to leave the city of your comfort and go into the wilderness of your intuition. What you'll discover will be wonderful. What you'll discover is yourself.

    — Alan Alda

Joy

You have it easily in your power to increase the sum total of this world's happiness now. How? By giving a few words of sincere appreciation to someone who is lonely or discouraged. Perhaps you will forget tomorrow the kind words you say today, but the recipient may cherish them over a lifetime.

    — Dale Carnegie

Judgment

We should look long and carefully at ourselves before we pass judgment on others.

—Molière

Kindness

We make a living by what we get, we make a life by what we give.

—*Winston Churchill*

Knowledge

An investment in knowledge pays the best interest.

—*Benjamin Franklin*

Laughter

Always laugh when you can. It is cheap medicine.

—Lord Byron

Laughter is the closest distance between two people.

—*Victor Borge*

The child in you, like all children, loves to laugh, to be around people who can laugh at themselves and life. Children instinctively know that the more laughter we have in our lives, the better.

—*Wayne Dyer*

Leadership

The challenge of leadership is to be strong, but not rude; be kind, but not weak; be bold, but not bully; be thoughtful, but not lazy; be humble, but not timid; be proud, but not arrogant, have humor, but without folly.

—*Jim Rohn*

Unless you're the lead dog, your view never changes.

—*Unknown*

A good leader inspires others with confidence in the leader, a great leader inspires them with confidence in themselves.

—*Unknown*

Learning

When the student is ready, the teacher will appear.

—*Buddhist reading*

Legacy

When you were born, you cried and the world rejoiced; live your life so that when you die, the world cries and you rejoice.

—*Cherokee Proverb*

Letting Go

We must give up last night in order for us to be ready for tonight.

—*Unknown*

Life

Life is a great big canvas, and you should throw all the paint on it you can.

>   —*Danny Kaye*

Life is not measured by the breaths you take, but the moments that take your breath away.

>   —*George Carlin*

When I hear somebody sigh that life is hard, I am always tempted to ask, "Compared to what?"

>   —*Sydney J. Harris*

Life is like an onion; you peel it off one layer at a time, and sometimes you weep.

>   —*Carl Sandburg*

Listening

Courage is what it takes to stand up and speak; courage is also what it takes to sit down and listen.

>   —*Winston Churchill*

Love

Love is unconditional commitment to an imperfect person.

>   —*Unknown*

When we cannot get what we love, we must love what is within our reach.

>   —*French Proverb*

Love. Love. Love. Then, Love some more.

–*Ginny Hutchinson*

Luck

The person afraid of bad luck will never know good.

–*Russian Proverb*

Magic

That's the thing with magic. You've got
to know it's still here, all around us,
or it just stays invisible for you.

–*Charles de Lint*

Mastery

Big shots are only little shots who keep shooting.

–*Christopher Morley*

Meditation

Meditation brings wisdom; lack of meditation leaves ignorance.
Know well what leads you forward and what holds you back,
and choose the path that leads to wisdom.

–*Buddha*

Relax your body and mind and let your Spirit soar high.

–*Unknown*

Mentoring

To the world, you may be just one person, but to one person you may be the world.

—*Brandi Snyder*

Miracle

The miracle is not to fly in the air, or walk on the water, but to walk on the earth.

—*Chinese Proverb*

Misfortune

The longer we dwell on our misfortunes, the greater is their power to harm us.

—*Voltaire*

Mission

Here is a test to find out whether your mission on earth is finished: If you are alive, it isn't.

—*Richard Bach*

Mistakes

The greatest mistake you can make, is to be continually afraid of making one.

—*Elbert Hubbard*

Modesty

Modesty is the best policy.

—*Cathy Haffner*

Money

Money is like water: It's best when clear, and it needs to flow freely or it can stagnate.

—*Kris Gopalakrishnan*

Music

One good thing about music, when it hits you, you feel no pain.

—*Bob Marley*

Where words fail, music speaks.

—*Hans Christian Andersen*

Mystery

I would rather live in a world where my life is surrounded by mystery than live in a world so small that my mind could comprehend it.

—*Harry Emerson Fosdick*

Nature

Look deep into nature, and then you will understand everything better.

—*Albert Einstein*

See how nature—trees, flowers, grass—grows in silence; see the stars, the moon and the sun, how they move in silence… we need silence to be able to touch souls.

—*Mother Teresa*

Neighbors

Man's greatest blunder has been in trying to make peace with the skies instead of making peace with his neighbors.

—*Elbert Hubbard*

Nurture

Today is the day to invest in those people we hope will call us "old friend" in the years to come.

—*Grant Fairley*

Openness

The mind is like a parachute. It works best when it is open.

—*Unknown*

Optimism

An optimist sees an opportunity in every calamity; a pessimist sees a calamity in every opportunity.

—*Sir Winston Churchill*

HALF EMPTY?

HALF FULL?

Opportunity

Opportunity is missed by most people because it is dressed in overalls and looks like work.

—*Thomas Edison*

Pain

Pain is temporary, pride is forever.

> —*Running mantra*

Parents

Always be nice to your children because they are the ones who will choose your rest home.

> —*Phyllis Diller*

Partnership

The easiest kind of relationship is with ten thousand people, the hardest is with one.

> —*Joan Baez*

Patience

Patience is the companion to wisdom.

> —*Saint Augustine*

The key to everything is patience. You get the chicken by hatching the egg—not by smashing it.

> —*Arnold Glasgow*

Peace

Each one has to find his peace from within. And peace to be real must be unaffected by outside circumstances.

> —*Mahatma Gandhi*

Performance

Whenever you take a step forward, you are bound to disturb something.

—*Indira Gandhi*

Perseverance

Don't give up. Keep going. There is always a chance that you will stumble onto something terrific. I have never heard of anyone stumbling over anything while he was sitting down.

—*Ann Landers*

Fall seven times, stand up eight.

—*Japanese Proverb*

Persistence

In the confrontation between the stream and the rock, the stream always wins... not through strength, but through persistence.

—*Buddha*

Perspective

The man who views the world at fifty the same as he did at twenty has wasted thirty years of his life.

—*Muhammad Ali*

Philanthropy

You must give some time to your fellow men. Even if it's a little thing, do something for others—something for which you get no pay but the privilege of doing it.

−Albert Schweitzer

Plan

It pays to plan ahead. It wasn't raining when Noah built the ark.

−Unknown

Planet Earth

Treat the earth well.
It was not given to you by your parents.
It was loaned to you by your children.
We do not inherit the earth from our ancestors,
We borrow it from our children.

−Native American Proverb

Play

It's good to play, and you must keep in practice.

−Jerry Seinfeld

The supreme accomplishment is to blur the line between work and play.

−Arnold Toynbee

Posture

Keep your head up and don't let anything get to you. Always keep good posture.

—Dante Bichette, Jr.

Praise

Appreciate everything your associates do for the business. Nothing else can quite substitute for a few well-chosen, well-timed, sincere words of praise. They're absolutely free and worth a fortune.

—Sam Walton

Preparation

One important key to success is self-confidence. An important key to self-confidence is preparation.

—Arthur Ashe

Present

Focus on the present. When the water is up to your chin, even a ripple can drown you.

—Chinese Proverb

Pride

Life loves to be taken by the lapel and told: "I'm with you kid. Let's go."

—Maya Angelou

Principles

When I do good, I feel good. When I do bad, I feel bad, and that is my religion.

—*Abraham Lincoln*

Problems

Our problems are our privileges. It's all the in way you view them.

—*Kate Stelter Belisle*

Procrastination

If I had my life to live again, I'd make the same mistakes, only sooner.

—*Tallulah Bankhead*

Possibilities

Don't go where the path may lead; go instead where there is no path.

—*Ralph Waldo Emerson*

Progress

If we never attempt things beyond what we've already mastered, we'll never grow.

—from The Princess Diaries

Promise

A rock pile ceases to be a rock pile the moment a single man contemplates it, bearing within him the image of a cathedral.

—*Antoine de Saint-Exupéry*

Purpose

Great souls are not those with fewer passions and more virtues than the ordinary run, but simply those with a stronger sense of purpose.

—*La Rochefoucauld*

Quest

Not everything that is faced can be changed, but nothing can be changed until it is faced.

—*James Baldwin*

Question

Quality questions create a quality life. Successful people ask better questions, and as a result, they get better answers.

—*Tony Robbins*

Quiet

Never be afraid to sit a while and think.

—*Lorraine Hansberry*

words to live by

Reading

Of all the diversions of life, there is none so proper to fill up its empty spaces as the reading of useful and entertaining authors.

—*Joseph Addison*

Rebellion

You can't shake hands with a clenched fist.

—*Indira Gandhi*

Recovery

Suffering isn't ennobling, recovery is.

—*Christian Barnard*

Relationships

After God created the world, he made man and woman. Then, to keep the whole thing from collapsing, he invented humor.

—*Guillermo Mordillo*

Relax

The really happy person is the one who can enjoy the scenery on a detour.

—*Unknown*

Remedy

Don't find fault, find a remedy.

—*Henry Ford*

Results

Both tears and sweat are salty, but they render different results. Tears will get you sympathy; sweat will get you change.

–Jesse Jackson

Rest

Retreat can move you forward.

–Unknown

Risk

He who is not every day conquering some fear has not learned the secret of life.

–Ralph Waldo Emerson

Sacrifice

Happiness can be defined, in part at least, as the fruit of the desire and ability to sacrifice what we want now for what we want eventually.

–Stephen R. Covey

Saving

The time to save is now. When a dog gets a bone, he doesn't go out and make a down payment on a bigger bone. He buries the one he's got.

–Will Rogers

Secrets

If you reveal your secrets to the wind you should not blame the wind for revealing them to the trees.

—*Khalil Gibran*

Self

The easiest thing in the world to be is you. The most difficult thing to be is what other people want you to be. Don't let them put you in that position.

—*Leo Buscaglia*

Self-confidence

I figured that if I said it enough, I would convince the world that I really was the greatest.

—*Muhammad Ali*

Serenity

First be at peace within yourself, then you can also bring peace to others.

—*Thomas à Kempis*

Service

The rich man is not one who is in possession of much, but one who gives much.

—*Saint John Chrysostom*

Silence

Let us be silent, that we may hear the whispers of the gods.

—Ralph Waldo Emerson

Silence is a source of great strength.

—Lao Tzu

Simplify

Our life is frittered away by detail... Simplify, simplify.

—Henry David Thoreau

Smile

If you see a friend without a smile,
give him one of yours.

—Proverb

Don't cry because it's over. Smile because it happened.

—Dr. Seuss

Smile... even when your life is at its worst. You never know
when you'll meet the one who takes your breath away.

—Jessica Biel

Too often we underestimate the power of a touch, a smile, a
kind word, a listening ear, an honest compliment, or the small-
est act of caring, all of which have the potential to turn a life
around.

—Leo Buscaglia

Solitude

A small period of solitude each day is a remarkable thing.

—Unknown

Soul

Let us be grateful to people who make us happy; they are the charming gardeners who make our souls blossom.

—Marcel Proust

Sorrow

When a good man is hurt, all who would be good must suffer with him.

—Euripedes

Strength

If you want to be strong, know your weaknesses.

—Unknown

Start Over

Nobody can go back and start a new beginning, but anyone can start today and make a new ending.

—Maria Robinson

Stress

I'm an old man who has known a great many problems, most of which never happened.

—Mark Twain

For fast acting relief, try slowing down.

　　　—Lily Tomlin

Strive

I am seeking. I am striving. I am in it with all
my heart.

　　　—Vincent van Gogh

Success

Success is not counted by how high you have
climbed but by how many people you brought with you.

　　　—Wil Rose

God gave us two ends. One to sit on and one to think with.
Success depends on which one you use; heads, you win—tails,
you lose.

　　　—Unknown

Surprise

My life has no purpose, no direction, no aim, no meaning, and
yet I'm happy. I can't figure it out. What am I doing right?

　　　—Charles Schultz

Sympathy

There is nothing sweeter than to be sympathized with.

　　　—George Santayana

Talent

Use the talents you possess. The woods would be very silent if no birds sang there except those that sang best.

—*Henry van Dyke*

Team

The way a team plays as a whole determines its success. You may have the greatest bunch of individual stars in the world, but if they don't play together, the club won't be worth a dime.

—*Babe Ruth*

Tenacity

Let me tell you the secret that has led me to my goal. My strength lies solely in my tenacity.

—*Louis Pasteur*

Thanks

No duty is more urgent than that of returning thanks.

—*James Allen*

Thinking

The significant problems we face today cannot be solved at the same level of thinking we were at when we created them.

—*Albert Einstein*

Thoughts

Life is a mirror and will reflect back to the thinker
what he thinks into it.

—*Ernest Holmes*

Time

You have exactly the same number of hours per day that were
given to Helen Keller, Louis Pasteur, Michelangelo, Mother Teresa,
Leonardo da Vinci, Thomas Jefferson, and Albert Einstein.

—*H. Jackson Brown, Jr.*

Transformation

You must want to fly so much that you are willing to give up
being a caterpillar.

—*Trina Paulus*

Travel

A journey is like marriage. The certain way to be wrong is to
think you control it.

—*John Steinbeck*

Triumph

I believe that imagination is stronger than knowledge—myth
is more potent than history—dreams are more powerful than
facts—hope always triumphs over experience—laughter is the
cure for grief—love is stronger than death.

—*Robert Fulghum*

words to Live By

Trust

Self-trust is the first secret of success.

—Ralph Waldo Emerson

Trust yourself. You know more than you think you do.

—Benjamin Spock

Truth

Truth is always exciting. Speak it, then;
life is dull without it.

—Pearl S. Buck

There is no weapon more powerful in achieving the truth than
acceptance of oneself.

—Swami Prajnanpad

Understanding

A friend is someone who understands your past, believes in
your future, and accepts you just the way you are.

—Unknown

Values

There is no right way to do a wrong thing.

—Unknown

Victory

Regardless of how you feel inside, always try to look like a winner. Even if you are behind, a sustained look of control and confidence can give you a mental edge that results in victory.

—*Arthur Ashe*

Virtue

What lies behind us and what lies before us are tiny matters compared to what lies within us.

—*Ralph Waldo Emerson*

Vision

Your vision will become clear only when you look into your own heart. Who looks outside, dreams. Who looks inside, awakens.

—*C. G. Jung*

Wake-up Calls

In the absence of wake-up calls, many of us never really confront the critical issues of life.

—*Stephen Covey*

words to live by

Wealth

Wealth is not his that has it, but his who enjoys it.

—*Benjamin Franklin*

It is wealth to be content.

—*Lao-Tzu*

Winning

As long as you keep a person down, some part of you has to be down there to hold him down, so it means you cannot soar as you otherwise might.

—*Marian Anderson*

Wisdom

You can tell whether a man is clever by his answers. You can tell whether a man is wise by his questions.

—*Naguib Mahfouz*

Work

To love what you do and feel that it matters—how could anything be more fun?

—*Katharine Graham*

We become what we do.

—*Madame Chiang Kai-Shek*

Nothing will work unless you do.

—*Maya Angelou*

Worry

Worry is the misuse of your imagination.

—Unknown

Youthfulness

You can't help getting older, but you don't have to get old.

—George Burns

Zeal

I'm in love with the potential of miracles. For me, the safest place is out on a limb.

—Shirley MacLaine

Zen

Zen does not confuse spirituality with thinking about God while one is peeling potatoes. Zen spirituality is just to peel the potatoes.

—Alan W. Watts

words to live by

...further explorations

On the Scottish Himalaya Expedition
By W. H. Murray

Until one is committed, there is hesitancy, the chance to draw back, always ineffectiveness. Concerning all acts of initiative and creation, there is one elementary truth the ignorance of which kills countless ideas and splendid plans: that the moment one definitely commits oneself, then providence moves too. All sorts of things occur to help one that would never otherwise have occurred. A whole stream of events issues from the decision, raising in one's favor all manner of unforeseen incidents, meetings and material assistance which no man could have dreamed would have come his way. I have learned a deep respect for one of Goethe's couplets: "Whatever you can do, or dream you can, begin it! Boldness had genius, magic and power in it."

Desiderata
By Max Ehrmann

Go placidly amid the noise and the haste, and remember what peace there may be in silence. As far as possible without surrender to be on good terms with all persons.

Speak you truth quietly and clearly; and listen to others, even to the dull and the ignorant, they too have their story. Avoid loud and aggressive persons; they are vexations to the spirit.

If you compare yourself to others, you may become vain and bitter, for always there will be greater and lesser persons than yourself.

Enjoy your achievements as well as you plans. Keep interested in your own career, however humble; it is a real possession in the changing fortunes of time.

Exercise caution in your business affairs, for the work is full of trickery. But let not this blind you to what virtue there is; many persons strive for high ideals, and everywhere life is fill of heroism.

Be yourself. Especially do no feign affection. Neither be cynical about love; for in the face of all aridity and disenchantment it is perennial as the grass. Take kindly the counsel of the years, gracefully surrendering the things of youth.

Nurture strength of spirit to shield you in sudden misfortune. But do not distress yourself with dark imaginings. Many feats are born of fatigue and loneliness.

Beyond a wholesome discipline, be gentle with yourself. You are a child of the universe, no less than the trees and the stars; you have a right to be here. And whether or not it is clear to you, no doubt the universe is unfolding as it should.

Therefore, be at peace with God, whatever you conceive him to be, and whatever your labors and aspirations in the noisy confusion of life, keep peace in your soul. With all its sham drudgery and broken dreams; it is still a beautiful world.

Be cheerful. Strive to be happy.

Autobiography in 5 Chapters
By Portia Nelson

CHAPTER I
I walk down the street.
There is a deep hole in the sidewalk.
I fall in.
I am lost... I am helpless.
It isn't my fault.
It takes forever to find a way out.

CHAPTER II
I walk down the same street.
There is a deep hole in the sidewalk.
I pretend I don't see it.
I fall in again.
I can't believe I am in the same place.
But, it isn't my fault.
It still takes a long time to get out.

CHAPTER III
I walk down the same street.
There is a deep hole in the sidewalk.
I see it is there.
I still fall in . . . it's a habit.
My eyes are open.
I know where I am.
It is my fault.
I get out immediately.

CHAPTER IV
I walk down the same street.
There is a deep hole in the sidewalk.
I walk around it.

CHAPTER V
I walk down another street.

Copyright © 1993, by Portia Nelson, from the book *There's a Hole in My Sidewalk*. Reprinted with permission from Beyond Words Publishing, Hillsboro, Oregon.

Better Because... you :)

BETTER WAYS TO TEXT IT

:-D	Laughter
LOL	Laugh out loud
:@	Exclamation "What???"
|-O	Yawning
^5	High-five
N1	Nice one
NBD	No big deal
TTYL	Talk to you later
:)	Standard smile
:-)	With nose
:(	Sad or frown smile
(((H)))	Hugs
<3	Love & friendship
:-X	Kiss on the lips
;)	Winking smile
@>--;--	Rose
:-!	Foot in mouth

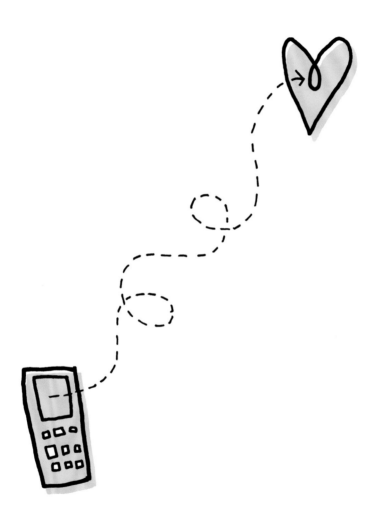

Better Because
Movement

better because...
you care

ONCE WE DECIDED to devote ourselves to building a positive movement, the first thing we did was make a donation to the Massachusetts Institute of Technology (MIT), focusing on ethics and leadership on behalf of Better Because.

Our ultimate dream is to start the Better Because Foundation to better the lives of people throughout the world through educational grants.

By supporting Better Because, you will help us realize this dream. Follow our progress on BetterBecause.com.

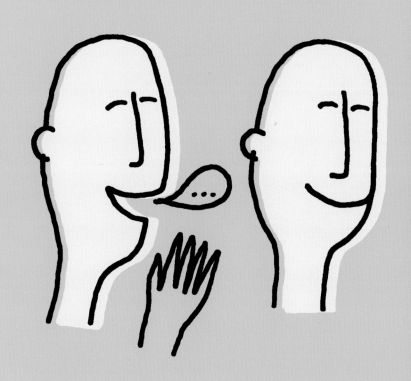

what's Next

better because...
you share

JOIN

Bookmark our web site, BetterBecause.com, to:

- ► Share your own Better Because story.
- ► Sign up for free weekly Better Life messages.
- ► Order additional copies of this book.

SHARE

Tell others about the Better Because book:

- ► Encourage your local bookstore to carry this book.
- ► Write a review on a commercial bookseller's site.
- ► Blog about Better Because.
- ► Ask your local newspaper to consider reviewing this book.

SUPPORT

Make the world a little bit better:

- ► Donate a copy of this book to your local library.
- ► Choose to participate in life.